Growing up Safe

Safety

poison

Illustrated by Sue Wilkinson

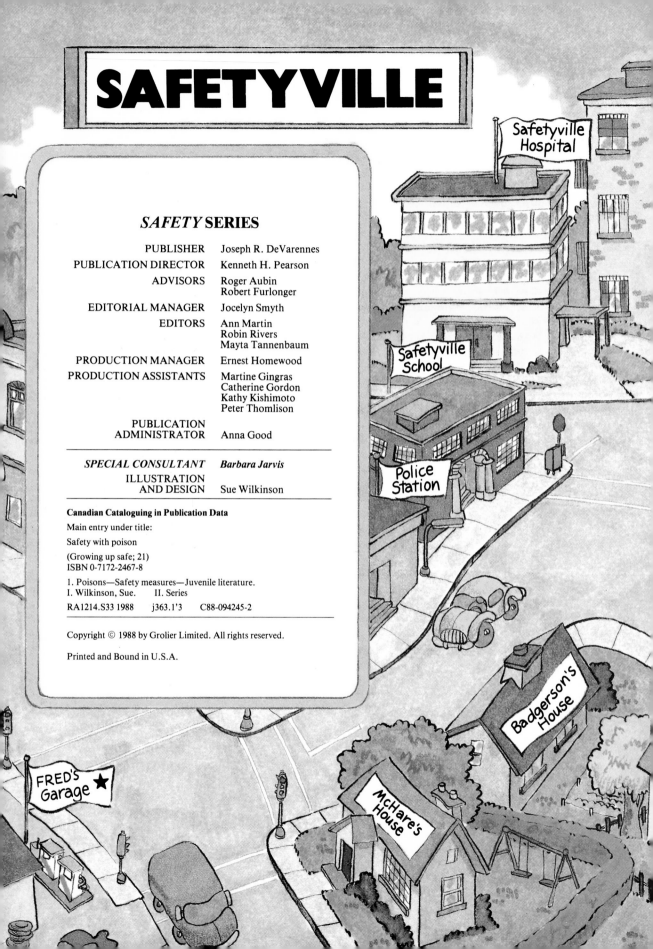

SAFETYVILLE

SAFETY SERIES

PUBLISHER	Joseph R. DeVarennes
PUBLICATION DIRECTOR	Kenneth H. Pearson
ADVISORS	Roger Aubin
	Robert Furlonger
EDITORIAL MANAGER	Jocelyn Smyth
EDITORS	Ann Martin
	Robin Rivers
	Mayta Tannenbaum
PRODUCTION MANAGER	Ernest Homewood
PRODUCTION ASSISTANTS	Martine Gingras
	Catherine Gordon
	Kathy Kishimoto
	Peter Thomlison
PUBLICATION ADMINISTRATOR	Anna Good

SPECIAL CONSULTANT	*Barbara Jarvis*
ILLUSTRATION AND DESIGN	Sue Wilkinson

Canadian Cataloguing in Publication Data

Main entry under title:

Safety with poison

(Growing up safe; 21)
ISBN 0-7172-2467-8

1. Poisons—Safety measures—Juvenile literature.
I. Wilkinson, Sue.   II. Series

RA1214.S33 1988   j363.1'3   C88-094245-2

Skunkerton Family

Mom   Alex Sarah

Come join Alex and Sarah Skunkerton as they find out everything they need to know about poison safety.

POISONS HAVE A SPECIAL SYMBOL.
DO NOT TOUCH CONTAINERS
WITH THIS SYMBOL.

POISONS ARE VERY DANGEROUS.
ONLY GROWNUPS SHOULD USE
POISONS.

CORROSIVES HAVE A SPECIAL SYMBOL. DO NOT TOUCH CONTAINERS WITH THIS SYMBOL.

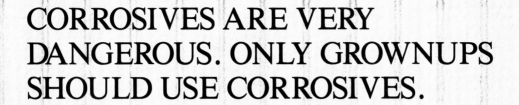

CORROSIVES ARE VERY
DANGEROUS. ONLY GROWNUPS
SHOULD USE CORROSIVES.

GROWNUPS KEEP MEDICINE IN A SPECIAL LOCKED CUPBOARD FOR SAFETY.

MEDICINE IS NOT CANDY. IT'S DANGEROUS TO TAKE MORE THAN THE RIGHT AMOUNT.

MANY INDOOR PLANTS ARE POISONOUS IF EATEN.

SOME OUTDOOR PLANTS ARE POISONOUS. CHECK WITH A GROWNUP BEFORE EATING ANY.

DO NOT TOUCH COSMETICS.
MANY OF THEM ARE POISONOUS.

KEROSENE AND GASOLINE ARE POISONOUS.

UNDER THE SINK IS NOT A SAFE
PLACE TO PLAY.

DO NOT TOUCH A CONTAINER WITHOUT A LABEL. IT MAY CONTAIN SOMETHING DANGEROUS.

DO NOT PLAY WITH GROWNUPS' PURSES OR BAGS. MANY DANGEROUS THINGS MAY BE INSIDE.

GARAGES ARE NOT SAFE PLACES TO PLAY. MANY DANGEROUS THINGS ARE STORED THERE.